ST. LOUIS
BLUES

BY CHRÖS MCDOUGALL

Book design by Maggie Villaume
Cover design by Maggie Villaume

Photographs ©: John Minchillo/AP Images, cover; Chris Szagola/Cal Sport Media/ZUMA Wire/AP Images, 4–5; Richard Ulreich/Cal Sport Media/AP Images, 7; Eric Canha/Cal Sport Media/ZUMA Wire/AP Images, 8; Bettman/Getty Images, 10–11; Fred Waters/AP Images, 12–13; Rusty Kennedy/AP Images, 14; Mark Elias/AP Images, 17; Mike Butkus/AP Images, 18–19; John Swart/AP Images, 20; James A. Finley/AP Images, 23; Jeff Roberson/AP Images, 24–25; Andy Clayton-King/AP Images, 27; Jack Dempsey/AP Images, 29

Press Box Books, an imprint of Press Room Editions.

ISBN
978-1-63494-595-0 (library bound)
978-1-63494-613-1 (paperback)
978-1-63494-648-3 (epub)
978-1-63494-631-5 (hosted ebook)

Library of Congress Control Number: 2022912935

Distributed by North Star Editions, Inc.
2297 Waters Drive
Mendota Heights, MN 55120
www.northstareditions.com

Printed in the United States of America
Mankato, MN
012023

ABOUT THE AUTHOR

Chrös McDougall is a sportswriter, editor, and author who often covers Olympic and Paralympic sports. A Minnesota native, he lives in Minneapolis with his wife, two kids, and an energetic boxer named Eira. His wife's family is from the St. Louis area, and they can tell you all about the 2019 Stanley Cup, too.

TABLE OF
CONTENTS

WORST
TO FIRST

The St. Louis Blues were done for. It was January 3, 2019. No National Hockey League (NHL) team had fewer points. Nothing was going right. So with nothing to lose, the team turned to a little-known goalie.

Jordan Binnington started his first NHL game on January 7. The Blues won in a shutout. The rookie won his next start, too. Before long, he was the main starter. And on

January 23, the Blues began an 11-game winning streak. Nine of those wins came with Binnington in goal. The Blues were clicking all over the ice. No team had more points after the new year. And by season's end, the Blues were comfortably in the playoffs.

St. Louis knew the playoffs well. In their history, the Blues had rarely missed the postseason. However, they had never finished as Stanley Cup champions. The red-hot 2018–19 Blues set out to change that.

Every series was intense. The second round, against the Dallas Stars, went to Game 7. Then it went to double overtime. Finally, St. Louis native Patrick Maroon

scored the winner. Nothing was going to stop the Blues from reaching the Stanley Cup Final.

Once there, only the Boston Bruins stood in the way of a championship.

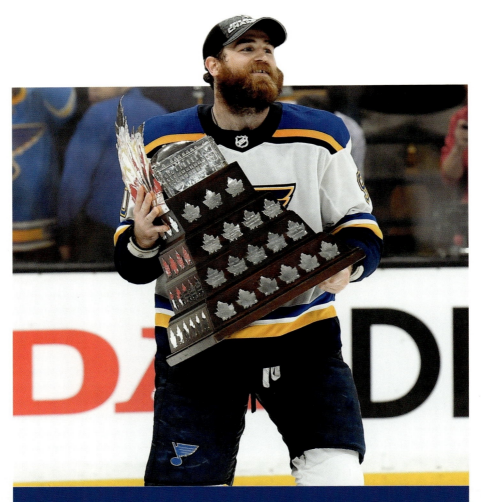

Ryan O'Reilly won the Conn Smythe Trophy as the best player in the 2019 playoffs. He had eight goals and 15 assists.

St. Louis would need all its stars to step up to win the series. No one rose up more than Ryan O'Reilly. The hard-nosed center was a beast on both ends of the ice.

His four goals helped push the series to Game 7 in Boston. Late in the first period, O'Reilly scored his fifth goal of the Final. Three minutes later, captain Alex Pietrangelo added another.

There was indeed no stopping the Blues. With a 4–1 win, they completed one of the sport's most remarkable turnarounds. The Blues were finally champions.

• CHANGE IS GOOD

The Blues fired head coach Mike Yeo 19 games into the 2018–19 season. They hired assistant coach Craig Berube to replace him. Berube made the decision to play Jordan Binnington. That sparked the Blues' run from last place to the Stanley Cup. The 2018–19 Blues became the seventh team in league history to win the Cup after changing coaches during the season.

2

Goalie Glenn Hall played the last four seasons of his 18-year career in St. Louis.

HOT AND COLD

For 25 seasons, the NHL featured just six teams. Then, in 1967, the league doubled in size to 12. Many cities tried to join the league. St. Louis wasn't one of them. However, the Chicago Black Hawks' owner also owned an old arena in St. Louis. He convinced the NHL to put a team there. Just like that, the Blues were born. They were named

after a popular W. C. Handy song called "St. Louis Blues."

New sports teams often struggle. After all, the best players are already signed with teams. But the NHL's 1967 expansion had a twist. The six new teams were all put in a new division. That meant one of them would make the Stanley Cup Final.

Hall (with goalie stick) lies on top of teammate Al Arbour as they both try to block a shot in the 1968 Stanley Cup Final.

The new teams were built through an expansion draft. Chicago left veteran goalie Glenn Hall available. The Blues built their first squad around him. They also selected defenseman Al Arbour. Meanwhile, winger Red Berenson arrived in a midseason trade. Together they led the Blues all the way to the Cup Final.

The series didn't last long. They were swept by the Montreal Canadiens.

The Blues were back in the Cup Final in 1969 and 1970, too. But the original NHL teams were still too strong. Each time, St. Louis was swept in four games.

That marked the start of a decline for the Blues. The divisions changed in 1970–71. The newer teams no longer had a direct ticket to the Stanley Cup Final. St. Louis still made the playoffs more often than not. But playoff runs always ended early. Meanwhile, into the 1980s, the team faced financial problems. Rumors swirled that the team might move or even disband. Something needed to change—fast.

SCOTTY BOWMAN

Early in the 1967–68 season, the Blues took a chance. They promoted promising young assistant coach Scotty Bowman to head coach. In four seasons, Bowman led the team to three Stanley Cup Finals. Then he left in 1971 following a dispute. Bowman coached 26 more seasons with other teams. His 1,244 wins are an NHL record. Bowman also won nine Stanley Cups.

BERNIE FEDERKO

Many iconic players have donned the famous blue note jersey. Among them, Bernie Federko stands out. The Canadian center joined the Blues in 1976. Over the next 13 seasons, he became a consistent scoring threat. He recorded 352 goals, 721 assists, and 1,073 points in 927 games. All were Blues records at the time.

Despite his success, Federko wasn't super famous outside of St. Louis. Some of the game's greatest scorers ever also shined in the 1980s. But Federko's playmaking ability struck a note with Blues fans. Players like Federko and winger Brian Sutter also thrived during a difficult era in St. Louis. Many credit them with helping save the team.

After retiring, Federko became a broadcaster for Blues games. Finally, in 2002, he was enshrined in the Hockey Hall of Fame.

Bernie Federko tallied
101 points in 91 career playoff
games for the Blues.

3

Brett Hull scored 527 goals in 744 games with the Blues.

GO, BLUES, GO

The Blues began a playoff streak in 1980. But they weren't always a great team. Often they qualified with a losing record.

On March 7, 1988, St. Louis traded for Brett Hull. The son of NHL legend Bobby Hull, Brett was one of the hottest young forwards in hockey. His arrival sparked new life in the Blues. By 1989–90, Hull led the NHL in goals. He repeated the feat the next two seasons, too.

Curtis Joseph led the league in saves for three straight seasons while playing for St. Louis.

Around Hull, the Blues were building a new core of players. Center Adam Oates was one of the sport's all-time great playmakers. Winger Brendan

Shanahan was emerging as a dangerous power forward. Meanwhile, Curtis Joseph showed much promise in net. But there was one problem. The Blues just couldn't put together a deep playoff run.

A new core emerged during the later 1990s. That included standout defensemen Chris Pronger and Al MacInnis. Veteran goalie Grant Fuhr was strong in net. But the playoff struggles

•THE GREAT ONE IN THE GATEWAY CITY

The Blues had a strong team in 1995–96. Wayne Gretzky was looking to win a fifth Stanley Cup. It looked like a perfect match. St. Louis traded for Gretzky that February. Hockey's all-time scoring leader was 35 years old. But he could still take over. It was an exciting time in St. Louis. However, Gretzky left that offseason after another playoff disappointment.

continued. The Blues kept making the playoffs. Then they'd fall short of the Stanley Cup Final. To make matters worse, Hull left as a free agent in 1998.

In 1999–2000, things felt different. Forwards Pavol Demitra and Pierre Turgeon paced the offense. Pronger and MacInnis anchored the defense. St. Louis charged to a team-record 51 wins. That was enough to earn the team's first Presidents' Trophy. It's awarded to the best team in the regular season. But the Blues were upset in the first round of the playoffs.

Another great player arrived in 2001. Forward Keith Tkachuk was big and tough. He scored lots of goals. But the playoffs

Chris Pronger (44) and Al MacInnis (2) celebrate with Dallas Drake after Drake's goal in a 2001 game.

kept ending in disappointment. Finally, in 2006, the Blues missed out. Their playoff streak had ended. It was time to rebuild.

4

Paul Kariya played the last three seasons of his Hall of Fame career in St. Louis.

JUST A DREAM

St. Louis, long a proud hockey city, had grown stale. Crowds were slumping. The city needed something new to be excited about.

A new owner, Dave Checketts, took over the team in 2006. He set about rebuilding trust with the fans. That started with improving the team. Paul Kariya joined in 2007. He and fellow winger Keith Tkachuk provided veteran leadership.

Young forwards David Backes, T. J. Oshie, and David Perron all showed promise. Alex Pietrangelo was one of the league's brightest young defensemen. St. Louis returned to the playoffs in 2009. Then the Blues began a six-year playoff streak in 2012.

St. Louis enjoyed some great seasons during this streak. It won a team-record 52 games in 2013–14. Three years later, the Blues made a run

• LOVING THE OUTDOORS

The NHL recognized the St. Louis hockey tradition in awarding the Blues the 2017 Winter Classic. The outdoor game drew more than 46,000 fans to Busch Stadium. Vladimir Tarasenko scored twice in a 4–1 win over the Chicago Blackhawks. In 2022, the Blues played in another Winter Classic. This time they beat the Wild 6–4 in Minnesota.

Vladimir Tarasenko scored a goal in the 2022 Winter Classic in Minneapolis. At –10 degrees Fahrenheit (–23°C), it was the coldest game in NHL history.

to the conference finals. They had done that only one other time in the last 21 seasons. But in 2018, the Blues missed the playoffs again.

The Blues were reliant on Russian winger Vladimir Tarasenko. He was an elite scorer. But he needed help. Some key moves in the summer of 2018 looked to put the Blues over the top. Pat Maroon joined his hometown team. Perron returned for the second time. The big move came that July. St. Louis added center Ryan O'Reilly in a trade with the Buffalo Sabres.

Going into 2018–19, the Blues had missed the playoffs just nine times in their 50 seasons. Yet despite their talent, they sank to the bottom of the standings. Then the Blues surged. The dream run ended with the team's first Stanley Cup championship. And with O'Reilly leading

the way, the Blues stayed competitive. In 2022, they recorded their first playoff series win since lifting the Cup. The future, once again, appeared bright.

ST. LOUIS BLUES
QUICK STATS

FOUNDED: 1967

STANLEY CUP CHAMPIONSHIPS: 1 (2019)

KEY COACHES:

- Scotty Bowman (1967–1971), 110 wins, 83 losses, 45 ties

- Ken Hitchcock (2011–2017), 248 wins, 124 losses, 41 overtime losses

- Craig Berube (2018–), 156 wins, 80 losses, 36 overtime losses

HOME ARENA: Enterprise Center (St. Louis, MO)

MOST CAREER POINTS: Bernie Federko (1,073)

MOST CAREER GOALS: Brett Hull (527)

MOST CAREER ASSISTS: Bernie Federko (721)

MOST CAREER SHUTOUTS: Brian Elliott (25)

Stats are accurate through the 2021–22 season.

GLOSSARY

CAPTAIN
A team's leader.

DRAFT
An event that allows teams to choose new players coming into the league.

EXPANSION
The way leagues grow by adding new teams.

FREE AGENT
A player who can sign with any team.

OVERTIME
An additional period of play to decide a game's winner.

PROMOTED
Moved someone up to a higher level.

ROOKIE
A professional athlete in his or her first year of competition.

VETERAN
A player who has spent several years in a league.

TO LEARN
MORE

BOOKS

Davidson, B. Keith. *NHL*. New York: Crabtree Publishing, 2022.

Duling, Kaitlyn. *Women in Hockey*. Lake Elmo, MN: Focus Readers, 2020.

Graves, Will. *Ultimate NHL Road Trip*. Minneapolis: Abdo Publishing, 2019.

MORE INFORMATION

To learn more about the St. Louis Blues, go to **pressboxbooks.com/AllAccess**.

These links are routinely monitored and updated to provide the most current information available.

INDEX